D1604609

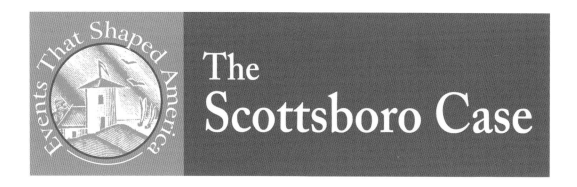

The
Scottsboro Case

Sabrina Crewe and Michael V. Uschan

Gareth Stevens Publishing

A WORLD ALMANAC EDUCATION GROUP COMPANY

Please visit our web site at: www.garethstevens.com
For a free color catalog describing Gareth Stevens Publishing's list of high-quality books and multimedia programs, call 1-800-542-2595 (USA) or 1-800-387-3178 (Canada). Gareth Stevens Publishing's fax: (414) 332-3567.

Library of Congress Cataloging-in-Publication Data

Crewe, Sabrina.
   The Scottsboro case / by Sabrina Crewe and Michael V. Uschan.
      p. cm. — (Events that shaped America)
   Includes bibliographical references and index.
   ISBN 0-8368-3407-0 (lib. bdg.)
   1. Scottsboro Trial, Scottsboro, Ala., 1931—Juvenile literature. 2. Trials (Rape)—Alabama—Scottsboro—Juvenile literature. I. Uschan, Michael V., 1948- . II. Title. III. Series.
   KF224.S34C74   2004
   345.73'02532'0976195—dc22   2004044240

This North American edition first published in 2005 by
Gareth Stevens Publishing
A World Almanac Education Group Company
330 West Olive Street, Suite 100
Milwaukee, WI 53212 USA

This edition © 2005 by Gareth Stevens Publishing.

Produced by Discovery Books
Editor: Sabrina Crewe
Designer and page production: Sabine Beaupré
Photo researcher: Sabrina Crewe
Maps and diagrams: Stefan Chabluk
Gareth Stevens editor: Jim Mezzanotte
Gareth Stevens art direction: Tammy West
Gareth Stevens production: Jessica Morris

Photo credits: AP/Wide World Photos: pp. 13, 17, 19, 21, 23, 25; Chicago Historical Society: p. 5; Corbis: cover, pp. 4, 6, 7, 8, 9, 10, 11, 14, 15, 18, 20, 22, 24, 26; Leroy Gist: p. 16; University of Virginia: p. 27.

Printed in the United States of America

1 2 3 4 5 6 7 8 9 09 08 07 06 05 04

Contents

Introduction

Haywood Patterson was one of the Scottsboro Boys. He was in prison from 1931 to 1947.

Arrest and Conviction

On March 25, 1931, nine young men were arrested when they were pulled off a train as it arrived in Paint Rock, Alabama. Just two weeks later, in the nearby town of Scottsboro, the young men—who became known as the Scottsboro Boys—were put on trial and found guilty of **rape**. Eight of them were sentenced to death.

The Scottsboro Case, however, was not about rape because no rape had taken place. It was about the **prejudice** that white Southerners had toward African Americans simply because they were black. In the 1930s, especially in the South, white Americans believed that African Americans were inferior and did not have the same rights as white people.

Color is Evidence
"If a white person says you did something, you did it. Color is more important than **evidence** down there. Color is evidence. Black color convicts you."

Haywood Patterson, one of the Scottsboro Boys,
Scottsboro Boy, *1950*

Years of Imprisonment

In the years following their **convictions**, the nine youths in the Scottsboro Case fought to prove their innocence. They were kept in prison, living in fear that they would be executed. Meanwhile, the Scottsboro Case was reported around the nation and the world. The coverage showed how Alabama's **racist** justice system denied the Scottsboro Boys their legal rights. People organized protests to call attention to the case, but it was years before the Scottsboro Boys were finally released.

Judge Callahan:—"I Instruct You to Bring in a Verdict in Accordance With the Laws of Alabama!"
Jury:—"We Git You, Judge"   —By Burck

Scottsboro Jury

Judge Callahan

Burck

In December 1933, the *Daily Worker* published this cartoon ridiculing the prejudice of the judge and jury in the Scottsboro Case. It didn't matter what the truth was—in Alabama, the Scottsboro Boys were guilty.

Names for Black People

In the South, white people used the term "boy" to address a black male, even an adult. The word "boy" was meant to humiliate African-American men by reminding them daily that white people did not respect them. An even cruder racist name commonly used in the 1930s was "nigger," a degrading form of "Negro." "Negro" or "colored" were more respectful terms, the equivalent of "African American," "person of color," or "black" today.

In the South

Chapter One

A movie house in Pensacola, Florida, in the 1930s had a separate entrance at the back for African Americans.

Segregation Replaces Slavery

In 1865, at the end of the Civil War, slavery was abolished in the United States. For some years, during a period called Reconstruction, the U.S. government tried to protect freed slaves in the South from white **discrimination**.

White Southerners, however, were just too powerful—they led the state governments and owned all the businesses and land. When Reconstruction ended in the 1870s, southern states began passing laws that denied African Americans such basic rights as being able to vote. The laws replaced slavery with **segregation**. Blacks could not eat in white restaurants, shop in white stores, attend white schools, or ride in the same train cars.

Living Under Segregation

There was little that southern blacks could do about segregation. African Americans could not vote and therefore could not elect leaders to help them. Whites refused to hire African Americans for anything but low-paying positions, such as laborers, cooks, or maids. In every way they could, white Southerners made sure African Americans were denied their **civil rights** and freedoms.

Southern Terrorists

Terrorists are people who use violence and threats against innocent people to achieve their goals. A group of terrorists called the Ku Klux Klan was formed in Tennessee in about 1865, and its goal was to prevent blacks from having equality and claiming their rights as citizens. At night, members of the Klan (shown below) would dress up in white hooded robes and terrorize black neighborhoods. They attacked African Americans, damaged and burned down houses, and left burning crosses as a symbol to frighten their victims.

The Ku Klux Klan and other racists also used **lynching** to terrorize black people. Groups of men would torture and then kill a person, usually by hanging. They would lynch an African American for stepping out of line in any way, such as speaking rudely, stealing food, or standing up to one of the many injustices inflicted on black people in daily life.

The NAACP issued this button to call public attention to the terrible practice of lynching.

Speaking Out

Racism existed in the rest of the United States, too, but in the northern states people were more **integrated** than in the South. People used the same public facilities, and some blacks could receive a good education and obtain decent jobs.

People in northern states, therefore, were able to speak out against the inequality suffered by their fellow African Americans in the South. One important fighter for racial equality was W. E. B. Du Bois, a Harvard University graduate. He worked tirelessly to improve the lives of African Americans by writing and speaking on the subject. In 1909, Du Bois helped found the National Association for the Advancement of Colored People (NAACP), which became the most powerful group working for African-American civil rights.

Full Rights

"We will not be satisfied to take one jot or tittle less than our full manhood rights. We claim for ourselves every single right that belongs to a free-born American, political, civil and social; and until we get these rights we will never cease to protest and assail the ears of America."

W. E. B. Du Bois, An ABC of Color, *1906*

The Great Depression

Despite the efforts of Du Bois and others, African Americans made little progress against racism, especially in the South. The Great Depression, which began in 1929 and lasted through the 1930s, made things even worse. In that period, a nationwide economic crisis caused extreme poverty and the loss of millions of jobs.

Black people had always held the worst jobs—the ones that were the hardest, dirtiest, and paid the least, such as washing dishes or digging ditches—because white people didn't want to do them. During the Great Depression, however, white people took any job they could get. When blacks had to compete with whites for jobs, they usually lost because of discrimination, and so the Great Depression made life even tougher for African Americans.

Sharecroppers farmed small plots of land and split the crop with their landlords. These sharecroppers lost their homes in the Great Depression, when many landowners needed the crops for themselves.

Chapter Two

On the Train

Riding the Freight Trains

During the Great Depression, people traveled long distances around the United States to look for work. They did not have any money, so many of them traveled for free by jumping on freight trains. People would ride in or on top of the railway cars that carried goods from one city to another.

On March 25, 1931, there were a number of illegal riders on a Southern Railroad freight train that left Chattanooga, Tennessee, for Memphis, Tennessee. Among the riders were the nine young men later known as the Scottsboro Boys. They were not all traveling together, and most of them did not know each other.

Travelers ride a freight train to Southern California in 1934. People who were homeless and traveled around in this way were known as "hoboes."

The Scottsboro Boys were (from left to right): Clarence Norris, Olen Montgomery, Andy Wright, Willie Roberson, Ozie Powell, Eugene Williams, Charlie Weems, Roy Wright, and Haywood Patterson.

A Fight on the Train

The train traveled along a route that dipped south into Alabama. Not long after the train passed Lookout Mountain in Alabama, a fight broke out between black and white riders. A group of whites ordered the blacks to get off because, they said, "This is a white man's train."

The claim was nonsense because all the travelers were illegally riding the train. But whites believed they had the right to order African Americans to do almost anything. When the blacks refused to get off, a fight broke out between seven white men and twelve black men. The African Americans won and threw some of the white riders off the train.

This map shows the towns where the Scottsboro Boys were arrested, jailed, and then tried over a period of many years.

Hang 'Em

"When the train arrived, it was immediately surrounded by a mob. There was nothing but white people with sticks, guns [and] pitchforks. Folks were hollering, 'Let's take them niggers off of there and put them to a tree and hang 'em.' All of us thought for sure we would be lynched right there, with no questions asked."

Clarence Norris, interviewed by Kwando Mbiassi Kinshasa, The Man from Scottsboro, *1980*

Paint Rock

The men who had been thrown off the train walked to the nearest station at Stevenson and told officials what happened. Angered that African Americans had beaten up whites, an official telegraphed to Paint Rock, Alabama, a train stop 38 miles (61 kilometers) away, so that the sheriff could arrest the blacks there.

When the train pulled into the small Paint Rock railroad station about 2:00 P.M., it was met by a group of seventy-five angry white men. Armed with pistols, shotguns, and other weapons, the group started pulling African Americans out of train cars. Many people riding the train, both black and white, escaped by running away from the angry mob. Nine young men were eventually caught and arrested. They were tied together, loaded on a truck, and driven to the nearby town of Scottsboro.

Charlie Weems, at twenty years old, was the oldest of the nine Scottsboro Boys. The youngest were Eugene Williams, thirteen, and Roy Wright, believed to be twelve. Roy's brother Andy Wright and Clarence Norris were nineteen years old; Haywood Patterson and Olen Montgomery were eighteen; Ozie Powell and Willie Roberson were both fifteen. The Wrights, Patterson, and Williams had known each other before they were arrested.

Willie Roberson (left) and Olen Montgomery (right).

The young men in the Scottsboro Case were typical of black Southerners in the 1930s—they had lived in poverty all their lives and were poorly educated. Eight were illiterate or nearly so. Haywood Patterson left school after the third grade, and the only job he had ever had was as a delivery boy. The mother of Charlie Weems died when he was four, and he was the only one of seven siblings to survive childhood. The others had similar difficult childhoods. Olen Montgomery—the only Scottsboro Boy who could read and write—was nearly blind in one eye, while Willie Roberson had trouble walking and had to use a cane.

Give Them All the Law Allows

"When I saw them nab those Negroes, I sure was happy. Mister, I never had a break in my life. Those Negroes have ruined me and Ruby forever. The only thing I ask is that they give them all the law allows."

Victoria Price, quoted in the Chattanooga Daily Times, *March 27, 1931*

The Two Women

When the sheriff's group searched the train cars in Paint Rock, they came upon two white women wearing overalls and caps. The two women identified themselves as twenty-one-year-old Victoria Price and seventeen-year-old Ruby Bates. They were on their way home to Huntsville, Alabama.

There are conflicting accounts about what the girls told law officers and who made the accusation. But finally one woman said, "We've been raped. All those colored boys raped us." The charge caused outrage. Not only was rape considered a horrible crime, but white Southerners believed a white woman having sex with a black man was one of the worst things that could happen. They considered this act so terrible because they believed the two races should remain separate.

Victoria Price on the witness stand during the Scottsboro trials. She would tell her story many times over a period of several years.

At Scottsboro Jail

As word spread that the nine African Americans had raped two white women, some five hundred angry white people gathered around the jail in Scottsboro. Many were members of the Ku Klux Klan. Some carried lengths of rope and screamed that they would kill the black men.

The Scottsboro Boys were terrified as the crowd surged around the jail all night. They had a good reason to be frightened. There had been twenty-one known lynchings in the South in the previous year.

Accused

The next day, the youths were taken from their cell to stand before the two women, Price and Bates, to be identified. Price pointed at six of them and said they had raped her. Bates was silent, but the law officers claimed that if Price had been raped, then Bates must have been, too.

The prisoners realized they were going to be charged with rape. They declared they had not harmed the women, but the law officers said they did not believe them. Clarence Norris said later that he realized at that moment he was in serious trouble.

As Good as Dead
"I knew if a white woman accused a black man of rape, he was as good as dead."

Clarence Norris, one of the Scottsboro Boys

On Trial

The Jackson County Courthouse in Scottsboro as it is today. In 1931, as the Scottsboro Boys arrived for their trials, the courthouse was surrounded by an angry crowd.

The Trials Begin

On April 6, 1931, a carnival atmosphere reigned in the streets around the Jackson County Courthouse in Scottsboro, Alabama. While a brass band played the popular Civil War song "Dixie," about eight thousand angry yet gleeful whites celebrated the start of the Scottsboro Boys' trial.

The Town of Scottsboro
"Scottsboro's just a little place:
No shame is write across its face—
Its courts too weak to stand against a mob,
Its people's heart, too small to hold a sob."

Langston Hughes, poet, Scottsboro Limited,
a book of poetry about the Scottsboro Case, 1932

Between April 6 and April 9, Judge A. E. Hawkins conducted the trials at a lightning pace. The Scottsboro Boys had **defense attorneys** to represent them, but one was usually drunk and the other was described as incompetent.

Victoria Price

In her **testimony**, Victoria Price told how a dozen African Americans threatened her and Bates with guns and knives and raped them. The other three attackers, she said, escaped when the train got to Paint Rock. Both women claimed six blacks raped each of them. Why did they lie? It is likely that the women were persuaded or forced to lie by local law officers. It is also possible that Price kept repeating her story for years afterward because she liked the attention and fame.

Other Testimony

Two local doctors, R. R. Bridges and Marvin Lynch, had examined the women after they got off the train. In their testimonies, both doctors noted that neither woman had the kind of bruises or other marks on their bodies that they should have had if their claims were true.

Victoria Price's Story

"There were six to me and three to her. One was holding my legs and the other had a knife to my throat. . . ."

Victoria Price, April 1931

Dr. R. R. Bridges testified in the Scottsboro trials in 1931 and again in 1933, when this picture was taken. Behind Dr. Bridges, Judge James Horton leans forward to hear the testimony.

Samuel Leibowitz (inside car) had body-guards to protect him everywhere he went in Alabama. White Southerners were very hostile toward him because he defended the Scottsboro Boys.

The Verdict

The **jury** found all the **defendants** guilty. Eight out of the nine were sentenced to death—Roy Wright didn't get the death sentence because one of the twelve jurors said he was too young.

Many people around the country believed the **verdict** was unfair and also thought the death sentences were too harsh. The lack of evidence cast doubt on whether the witnesses had told the truth, and many people also realized the defense attorneys had done their jobs badly.

Supporters of the Scottsboro Boys hired good attorneys, including criminal lawyer Samuel Leibowitz, to **appeal** the verdicts. On November 7, 1932, the **U.S. Supreme Court** agreed the trials had been unfair and ordered new trials.

The Southern Jury

The **jurors** at the Scottsboro trials were all white, as juries in the South always were in the 1930s. Their job was to listen to the evidence and then decide whether or not the person being tried was guilty. But the jury's prejudice, not the evidence, decided the verdict in the Scottsboro Case. The U.S. Supreme Court, however, made a famous **ruling** about the Scottsboro Case in 1935. It said the Scottsboro Boys had been denied a fair trial because the jury was all white, which was **unconstitutional**. After this ruling, African Americans began to be included in juries, even in the South.

Made to Lie

"Those policemen made me tell a lie that is my statement because I want to clear myself. . . . Those Negroes did not touch me or those white boys. I hope you will believe me the law don't."

Ruby Bates, letter to her boyfriend Earl Streetman, January 5, 1932

Bates Changes Her Story

The second trials began March 27, 1933, in Decatur, Alabama, before Judge James Horton. On April 6, 1933, Ruby Bates appeared at Haywood Patterson's trial, but this time as a witness for the defense. Everyone was amazed when Bates admitted that the defendants had not attacked her. Bates also said she was with Price the entire time they were on the train and that Price had not been raped, either.

Bates's new testimony made no difference. Once again, the jury ignored the facts and ordered the death sentence.

In 1933, Ruby Bates (center) took back her accusations of rape and tried to help the Scottsboro Boys. She is seen here with four of the Scottsboro Boys' mothers.

The Trials Go On

For more than six years after the fight on the train, the trials and appeals continued. People argued and appealed and protested about the Scottsboro Case. While the outside world sympathized, however, the Scottsboro Boys were treated very harshly in prison. As the years went by, they grew into men, holed up in tiny cells day after day, not knowing if they would be executed or released.

Protests

All over the United States and in other countries, too, newspapers condemned the trials. Even southern newspapers began to question why the trials went on for years. The *News Leader* in Richmond, Virginia, declared in April 1933: "The men are being sentenced to death primarily because they are black." Supporters of the Scottsboro Boys, who believed it was wrong that African Americans could not get a fair trial, held protests in many cities. In one large protest in Washington, D.C., several thousand African Americans marched to the gates of the White House to demand that President Franklin D. Roosevelt free the Scottsboro Boys.

The protest march to the White House was led by Mrs. Janie Patterson, mother of Haywood Patterson.

These 1937 photographs tell two different stories. Willie Roberson (far right) and Eugene Williams happily celebrate their freedom, but Haywood Patterson (far left) is left behind in Kilby Prison.

Dropped Charges

In 1937, a fourth round of trials had begun when something surprising happened. On July 24, the rape charges were dropped against five of the nine Scottsboro Boys. One of them, Ozie Powell, was held for having attacked a guard the year before, but the other four—Olen Montgomery, Roy Wright, Willie Roberson, and Eugene Williams—were freed.

Kilby Prison

"At Kilby, we were caged in narrow cells with small windows which prevented us from seeing anything except a few cells directly in front of you. We weren't allowed to leave our ten-by-twelve cells . . . you were always subject to being cursed at or beaten by the guards. They would always call you 'nigger this' and 'nigger that.'"

Clarence Norris, interviewed by Kwando Mbiassi Kinshasa,
The Man from Scottsboro, *1980*

What Happened?

The five left in prison were understandably angry and discouraged. As Norris said later, "It was the saddest day of my life."

Everyone else was just confused. If five were not guilty, people thought, then surely none were guilty. In an editorial, the *Times-Dispatch* in Richmond, Virginia, echoed popular opinion that the outcome of the latest trials was "a virtual clincher that all nine Negroes are innocent." Why, then, did only four go free?

A Compromise

The reason was that Alabama had, at last, grown weary of being portrayed as a state full of mean-spirited racists. The court was worried, however, that dropping all the charges would infuriate Southerners, and so it came up with a **compromise**. The four who appeared the most harmless were freed: the two youngest defendants, Eugene Williams and Roy Wright, along with Olen Montgomery and Willie Roberson, whose physical disabilities had always made them unlikely suspects.

The compromise included a promise that the others could be **paroled** as early as 1938. But on November 5, 1938, Governor Bibb Graves broke the promise and denied parole for the remaining Scottsboro Boys, claiming they were still dangerous. Not even a letter from President Franklin D. Roosevelt on December 7, 1938, urging parole, could sway him.

Freedom at Last

Four of the five prisoners were eventually paroled, but only after several years. Charlie Weems was freed in 1943, Clarence Norris and Andy Wright were freed in 1944, and Ozie Powell was released in 1946.

Haywood Patterson was never paroled. On July 17, 1947, however —sixteen years after his wrongful arrest—he led several other prisoners in an escape from a prison farm near Kilby Prison. Patterson made his way to freedom in Detroit, Michigan. When Alabama officials discovered where Patterson was and tried to have him returned to prison, Michigan governor G. Mennen Williams refused to send him back.

Escape
"We were thinning rice at that time, working in the rice field. . . . I got all the boys together and said, 'Let's go.' We hit for the woods. . . . I told the others, 'Get going. Go fast.'"

Haywood Patterson, describing his prison escape, Scottsboro Boy, *1950*

Thirteen years after his arrest, Clarence Norris walked out of Kilby Prison, paroled at last.

After the Trials

The South

Despite publicity about the Scottsboro Case, nothing changed in the way whites mistreated African Americans in the South. White people continued to keep black people segregated and deny many of their rights. The Ku Klux Klan continued to terrorize African Americans, beating and killing them for small or imagined offenses.

The Emmett Till Case

In 1955, fourteen-year-old Emmett Till from Chicago, Illinois, was visiting relatives in Money, Mississippi. In response to a dare by friends, he whistled at and spoke to Carolyn Bryant, a white woman. It was a harmless action, but on the night of August 28, several men with guns abducted him from the house where he was staying and beat him to death.

Ray Bryant, the woman's husband, and J. W. Milam were charged with murder. Despite testimony that showed they were guilty, a white jury **acquitted** them. The Scottsboro Case had shown that any black person charged with hurting a white was automatically guilty. The Till trial showed that white people who killed African Americans would not be punished.

Mose Wright identified his nephew Emmett Till's murderers in court, but the men were acquitted anyway.

Life for southern African Americans would not begin to change much until the civil rights movement began in the mid-1950s. Until then, thousands of innocent Americans like the Scottsboro Boys would continue to suffer at the hands of white racists.

The Scottsboro Boys

Most of the Scottsboro Boys led troubled lives after their release. They struggled to hold jobs, drank heavily, and got into more trouble. The Scottsboro Case had ruined their lives.

Clarence Norris was the only one of the Scottsboro Boys to receive a full pardon. He is shown here at a press conference at the time of his pardon in 1976.

Clarence Norris did better than the others—he moved to New York City, married, and raised a family. He also began the process of seeking a full pardon. On November 29, 1976, in Montgomery, Alabama, Norris finally received his pardon. By then, all the other Scottsboro Boys had died.

No Hate

"I have no hate toward any creed or color. I like all people, and I think all people accused of things which they didn't commit should be free. I wish these other eight boys were around because their lives were ruined by this thing too."

Clarence Norris, after accepting his pardon, November 29, 1976

Conclusion

Thurgood Marshall (top right) was the first African American appointed to the U.S. Supreme Court. This photograph of the justices was taken to mark Marshall's appointment in 1967.

A Television Show

By 1976, when Clarence Norris received his pardon, the Scottsboro Case had faded into obscurity. That year, however, the NBC television network broadcast a show about the case. Victoria Price had married a tobacco farmer in Flintville, Tennessee, and was now known as Katherine Victory Street. When the show was aired, she filed a libel lawsuit because it portrayed her as a person with bad morals. (Ruby Bates also filed a lawsuit, but she died before it was settled.) Street used the money she got from NBC to buy a small house, something she said had always been her dream. She died without ever apologizing for ruining so many lives with her lies.

Presumed Guilty

The color of their skin was enough to convict the Scottsboro Boys of a crime they did not commit. In their case, justice did not matter as much as the fact that they were black. In 1931, their color meant they must be guilty of anything a white person accused them of doing.

Race and Justice Today

More than seventy years later, the color of a person's skin still influences the U.S. criminal justice system. African Americans make up only about 12 percent of the nation's population. But there are nearly as many blacks in jails and prisons as there are whites, who form a much larger percentage of the U.S. population. Poverty and living conditions are partly to blame, but racial discrimination is also a factor. For example, it seems African Americans have been unfairly targeted in the nation's war on drugs. There are many more white than black drug users, but about 62 percent of prisoners held on drug charges are African Americans and only 36 percent are whites.

Justice
"That Justice is
a blind goddess
Is a thing to which
we black are wise.
Her bandage hides
two festering sores
That once perhaps
were eyes."

Langston Hughes, poet,
Scottsboro Limited,
*a book of poetry
about the Scottsboro
Case, 1932*

Time Line

1909	NAACP is founded.
1929	Great Depression begins.
1931	March 25: Nine youths are arrested in Paint Rock, Alabama, and accused of rape (March 26).
	April 6: Scottsboro Case trials begin.
	April 7–9: Scottsboro Boys are tried, convicted, and sentenced to death.
	June 22: Executions are put on hold pending appeal to Alabama Supreme Court.
1932	January 5: Ruby Bates admits she was not raped in a letter to her boyfriend, Earl Streetman.
	November 7: U.S. Supreme Court reverses Scottsboro Case convictions in *Powell v. Alabama* and orders new trials.
1933	March 27: Second round of trials begin.
	April 9: Haywood Patterson is found guilty again and sentenced to death.
1935	April 1: U.S. Supreme Court reverses latest Scottsboro Case convictions in *Patterson v. Alabama*.
1936	January 24: Ozie Powell stabs deputy sheriff.
1937	July 24: Roy Wright, Eugene Williams, Olen Montgomery, and Willie Roberson are released.
1938	November 5: Alabama governor Bibb Graves denies parole to Scottsboro Boys remaining in prison.
1943	Charlie Weems is released.
1944	Clarence Norris and Andy Wright are released.
1946	Ozie Powell is released.
1947	Haywood Patterson escapes from prison.
1955	Murder of Emmett Till.
1976	November: Clarence Norris is pardoned by Alabama governor George Wallace.

Things to Think About and Do

Segregation

Find out what you can about life for black people in the South in the time of segregation. List the things you find that deprived African Americans of their rights. Think about how their lives compare with yours, especially in terms of the basic rights and freedoms that you take for granted.

Prisoner

Imagine you are one of the Scottsboro Boys, and write a journal covering a few days of your life while in prison. You could include a typical day's experience as a prisoner, a day in court, and maybe the day you were released.

Glossary

acquit: pronounce a person not guilty of a crime.

appeal: ask a higher court to examine a trial verdict and overturn it.

civil rights: basic rights—such as the right to vote—of every person.

compromise: agreement or decision that reflects the concerns of both sides.

conviction: declaration that a person is guilty of a crime.

defendant: person charged with a crime.

defense attorney: legal representative who speaks in favor of a defendant.

discrimination: showing of preference for one thing over another. Racial discrimination happens when one racial group is given preference over another racial group.

evidence: something used as proof, especially in a court of law.

integrate: mix together people of different races.

juror: person who sits on a jury in a court of law.

jury: people in a court who decide if an accused person is guilty.

lynching: torture and murder of a person by a group of people, usually by hanging.

parole: allow a person to leave prison before finishing his or her sentence.

prejudice: bias against someone because of race or other factors.

racist: having opinions about a person based on his or her race.

rape: crime of forcing another person to perform a sex act.

ruling: decision of a judge or panel of judges.

segregation: separation of people of different races.

testimony: words of a person given in evidence at a trial.

unconstitutional: action or law that goes against the U.S. Constitution.

U.S. Supreme Court: highest court in the United States, which makes final decisions on matters of law and interpretation of the U.S. Constitution.

verdict: decision made by the jury in a trial.

Further Information

Books

Koestler, Rachel A. *Going to School During the Civil Rights Movement* (Going to School in History). Blue Earth, 2001.

Santella, Andrew. *The NAACP: An Organization Working to End Discrimination* (Journey to Freedom). Child's World, 2003.

Sorenson, Lita. *The Scottsboro Boys Trial: A Primary Source Account*. Rosen, 2003.

Wormser, Richard. *The Rise and Fall of Jim Crow*. St. Martin's, 2003.

Web Sites

www.law.umkc.edu/faculty/projects/FTrials/scottsboro/scottsb.htm
University of Missouri web site about the Scottsboro Case covers everything from the legal decisions to the participants to the incident itself.

www.naacp.org The web site of the National Association for the Advancement of Colored People offers historical information and current news about African-American civil rights.

www.pbs.org/wgbh/amex/scottsboro Public Broadcasting System web site based on a television program about the Scottsboro Case includes pictures, official documents, and first-person accounts by the people involved.

Useful Addresses

National Association for the Advancement of Colored People
4805 Mt. Hope Drive
Baltimore, MD 21215
Telephone: (410) 521-4939

Index

Page numbers in **bold** indicate pictures.